Walk gently through the pages of
this book, for here you will find
many well worn paths, and some may
even bear your footprints. If you
should find a particular familar
path, do not hesitate to pause
long enough to say
    "I've been there before"

Sue Kampa

To Someone Very Special
  "Let's be Friends Forever"

To grow older
  is to grow more wise...
To see more
  through loving eyes
To feel more deeply
All the Joy a new day brings
  To look more closely
    at all the little happenings...
To treasure friends and flowers
            children at play

To listen what people "mean"
  as well as what they say
To have high respect for goodness
  and for truth...
Then growing older has the heart
  and soul of youth.

Think of Me

Think of me when you need a friend
And you find you want to share some
special dream or secret thought
with someone who will care...
Think of me when you're feeling blue
And you need a word of cheer
Or you've had a problem on your mind
That you wish someone would hear....
Think of me when you've just been blessed
With the richest joys you've had
It could only bring more happiness
To know someone was glad...
Think of me as the days go by
And remember as you do
Your thoughts will all be greeted by
My own warm thoughts of you.

A Love Poem

Sometimes it is hard to express my
thoughts,
But he understands my silence.
Sometimes it is hard to express my
sorrow,
But he understands my tears.
Sometimes it is hard to express my
Happiness,
But he understands my laughter.
Yet it is always easy to say,
"I love you,"
and he understands this, too.

The most beautiful
gift
we can give
each other
is the truth.

A Tear

A tear
One solitary drop
filled with
overflowing emotion
revealing
something deep within
from the heart
soul.
A symbol of love, joy
fear,
sorrow.
So simple, small:
yet overpowering.
So uncomplicated
in this world
of confusion.

The most
I can do for
my friend is
simply to be
his friend.

Please hang on
to whatever it is that helps you be
who you are and how you are
and still lets you see
who I am and where I am

Time has come again
And love is in the wind
Like some music in a dream
You made them all come true
When you came inside my life

Now I'm lost
Inside of you
Lost in the music
And lost in your eyes
I could spend all of my time
Hearing songs you sing
Feeling love you bring
Darling being close to you
Made all me dreams come true
When you came inside my life
Now I'm lost inside of you.

I do my thing, and you do your thing.
I am not in this world to live up to your
expectations.
And you are not in this world to live up
to mine.
You are you and I am I.
And if by chance we find each other,
it's beautiful.

Only If Your Love Dies

Don't leave me for another
Don't leave me because of something I said.
Just leave me if your love for me has died.
Sure, I'll still love you, but love works two ways.
Once one dies, the other has nothing to live for.
So once you leave me, I'll get over it;
But in my heart there'll always
be a place for your love.
So remember:
Don't leave me for another.
Don't leave me because of something I said.
Just leave me if your love for me dies.

Gather my Love

Gather my love
Into bright golden baskets
And cherish it close by
Your heart.
Gather my love
And protect it forever,
Yet respect both myself and
my love.
Gather my love
But gather it slowly,
For time is the master
of love.

Honest Feelings

On the day I saw you, I hoped that
you'd be mine and with each passing day
I hope its only a matter of time till that day
I guess that I'll just wait around to see. if
by any chance you just might feel the same
of me. Other guys may come and go
young love usually doesn't last long.

But for guys like you; the feeling
always burns strong. other girls may
tempt you! with their fast and phoney
plays. but me, I guess I'm just to real
to try those out on ways. So if the day
should ever come that you would turn
to me I hope it would be for just
myself, not for something. I couldn't be.

Love is like a butterfly....it goes wherever it pleases and pleases wherever it goes

Thoughts on Friendship

There is nothing in this world
Lord like having one true friend. Just
one true enjoyable, understanding friend.

No one is even so lonely that he doesn't
have a friend. To find one all you have to
do is go out and help somebody.

Now and then say to a friend "I love you."
Those words weren't meant only for
sweethearts. They are just as significant,
beautiful and life chancing when said to
a dear friend.

If you want more friends smile more!
I've never known anyone who smiled
a lot who didn't have any friends.

Friends are too precious to lose - even
when they dissapoint us Lord. Help me
to forgive this friend - if only because
I love and need them to forgive me
Friends are worth forgiving.

Things do not change,
we change

Rushing Through Life

Take time to think - thoughts are the
    source of power.

Take time to play - play is the secret
    of perpetual youth.

Take time to read - Reading is the
    fountain of wisdom.

Take time to pray - prayer can be a
    rock of strength in time of trouble.

Take time to love - loving is what
    makes living worthwhile.

Take time to be friendly - Friendships
    give life a delicious flavor.

Take time to laugh - laughter is
    the music of the soul.

Take time to give - any day of the
    year is too short for selfishness.

Take time to do your work well - pride
    in your work. no matter what it is,
    nourishes the ego and the spirit.

Take time to show appreciation -
    thanks is the frosting on the cake of life.

Spectrum of Love

"I love you"

There is a much greater motivation than simply my spoken words. For me to love, is to commit myself, freely and without reservation. I am sincerely interested in your happiness and wellbeing. Whatever your needs are I will try to fulfill them and will bend in my values depending on the importance of your needs. If you are lonely and need me. I will be there. If in that loneliness you need to talk, I will listen. If you need to listen, I will talk. If you need the strength of human touch, I will touch you. If you need to be held, I will hold you. I will lie naked in body with you if that be your need. If you need fulfillment of the flesh, I will give you that also, but only through my love.

I will try to be constant with you so that you will understand the core of me of my personality and from that understanding you can gain strength and security that I am acting as me. I may faulter with my moods. I may project, at times, a strangeness that is alien to you which may bewilder or frighten you. There will be times when you question my motives. But because people are never constant and are as changeable as the seasons, I will try to build up within you a faith in my fundamental attitude

Laughter through our tears

Sometimes we sit
    Thinking
Staring off into the liquid sunset;
Tears slowly creep down our faces.

Alone we sit
Knowing that waves of life
have crashed us into a stone wall
of hurt and happiness

No one sees the tears
No one knows the pain.
They see only the smiles
Listening to merry laughter
As we pretend
That nothing ever goes wrong
But inside
Where our feelings live
And our true being resides,
We know it's only
Laughter through our tears.

Kindness
    is the
    overflowing
        of
    oneself
        into
the lives
    of others

magic is the
    key to
most peoples dreams
Determination is the
    key to mine

The human race
    has one
really effective
weapon and
    that is
laughter

apart and free
not by desire
or I... nor thee...
Together... not free
    forever
        In thought.
        In faith
        In love
    Are we...

Love and friends

A message of love   friendship
Is sent with d___ion and care.
especially for ___ery dear friend
Loving wishes with you I share.
True friend ___re few and priceless,
for you I ___ill always care.
In times ___f anxiety and stress
my tho___ts and prayers are there.

       He who
Would live in Peace
    And at ease
Must not speak
   All He knows,
    Nor judge
   all he sees.

What sunshine is to flowers,
smiles are to humanity. They are
but trifles to be sure; but scattered
along life's pathways, the good
they do is inconceivable.

frienship

frienship is a word
  bringing many thoughts to mind.
With careful giving of yourself
you'll see it's easy to find.

frienship is the giving
  of faith hope, joy and love.
To all who need and cherish it
  its like a star from above.

So, for all who wish to give to you
  the one most precious gift,
Smile and accept it graciously —
  it can be a most welcome lift.

There is no need for
an outpouring of words
to explain oneself
to a friend.
Friends understand each
others thoughts even
before they are spoken.

Because our relationship
is based on
honesty and
fairness
there is no
need to test
each other.
It is so
wonderful
to find someone
who I
don't need
to play games
with
and who lives
up to everything that
I consider
important, right and
beautiful.

Across the sea of sunny hopes
With loads of wishes true
A little ship of kindly thoughts
Goes on its way to you —
And it will sail right on and on.
Allowing no delays
Until it brings you to the port
Of warm and happy days.

What are tears —
Tears are only shadows
of feelings deep inside.
Of secrets and of troubles
We're trying so to hide.
Tears are whisperings of sorrow
That fill the heart and soul;
They weave the web of wearness
And make the saddness show
Tears are really cries for help,
Their silent echo weeps;
They wash the windows of the soul
And close the mind that seeks.

To be loved

To be admired, is a wish... but
To be loved... is to accomplish

Personality

The human personality
 Is very much a mystery;
It should never be taken too lightly
 Nor too seriously.
For the mirror of the mind is not
 always clear, and
The image upon the eye is sometimes
 full of fear.

The Little Things

The little things
are most worthwhile -
A quiet word,
A look, a smile,
A listening ear
That's quick to share
Another's thoughts
Another's care...
Though sometimes
they may seem
quite small,
These things
mean most of all.

A Wish

I wish you love, strength, faith, and
wisdom. Goods. golds enough to help
some needy one,
I wish you songs, but also blessed silence
and God's sweet peace when everyday
is done.

Sand Castles

I've built dreams of you
about,
    among,
        and around you.
Dreams
within my mind, made of sand.
Such castles I have built
All of life and living,
touched
with the golden rod of sunset,
with love
that held the grains together
But I forgot the tide,
that incoming, outgoing wave
which reduced my castles
to no more than a mass of sand.

If I were a ~~bird~~ bird
I'd be a mockingbird
and sing ever song ever written.

Very little is needed to make a happy life. It is all within yourself, in your way of thinking.

Marcus Aurelius

How beautiful a day can be when kindness touches it.

George Elliston

Just as there comes a warm sunbeam into every cottage window, so comes a love-beam of Gods care and pity for every separate need.

Nathaniel Hawthorne

The sun does not shine for a few trees and flowers, but for the wide worlds joy.

Henry Ward Beecher

Peace I leave with you; my peace I give to you, not as the world gives do I give to you. Let not your hearts be troubled, neither let them be afraid.

John 14:27 (RSVB)

You've Got a Friend

Someday may your days be bright,
Filled with an inner glowing light.
May you find such a peace within
To draw the line of emptiness thin
May the day come soon to your heart,
Proving you play a significant part.
May bounds of joy be always yours
To greet you at life's open doors.
May a friend or two be always near
To share and ease any hidden fear.
Always may God's beauty find
A place for storage in your mind.
May tender cares find their way
To loven up your every day.
Many wishes accompany these
To give your life much more peace and ease
All my wishes God may never send
But remember always: you've got a friend.

The Dream

Maybe someday in your own
space and time you'll find that one
special person

Lost Dream

You are my lost dream;
I love you so.
More and more each day
Than you'll ever know.

Oh how I wish you could be mine.
But as time goes by,
The hope that is in my heart
Is slowly fading away.

But each night I pray.
That I'll see you again someday.
With that wonderful look in your eyes.
I'll smile at you like I did before.
And promise you my love forevermore.

You are my lost dream;
I love you so.
More and more each day
Than you'll ever know.

Question

The world continues.
     We   grow
               and
                    learn.
Our hands
     become more
               skilled.
Our minds,
     more
          alert.
Why is
     it, then,
that we become
     afraid of love?

I Want to Understand

Gazing into your eyes... searching your face intently
    as if to penetrate your soul...
I don't mean to invade your privacy!
Very simply, I want to understand you
because I know you want to be understood!
Should we find that we are worlds apart
    in our values and views.
I will appreciate your individuality and
I will be most grateful to learn from you.
    Never could I criticize you for being
different!

    I would consider it a honor if you
would share with me the journeys you have
taken that have made you what you are.
    I do care!
And if we share the same values and
views...
    Just imagine the joy we could share
exploring the avenues of life together...
where once we walked alone
    Alone we create... together we enjoy
    the creation.

The Way to Live

live now for now —
day by day
today for tomorrow.
and not ❀ tomorrow
for today.

live today
for today is here;
yesterday is gone
and tomorrow
has not yet arrived.

The Test of Time

Trust
Is experiencing the unique feelings of warmth
And innocence of young love.
Trust
Is looking into another's eyes.
seeing the deep emotional loneliness,
The hidden desires of wanting
To give of one's self completely.

At night, when it is very still,
I think I am alone until
The little child I used to be
Comes in to sit and talk with me.
I see beyond her
all my forgotten yesterdays
I'm glad we know each other yet—
I and the child who can't forget.

On Reflection

A relationship is:
Two people, each doing their own thing.
Coming together
To share their hopes,
Their joys,
Their struggles
Their successes,
Their bodies,
And their spirits.
At times one,
But not always, and not always
in the same place.
Joining on many levels.
Yet separate and apart.
Free to be you,
And, free to be me.

Why, doesn't anyone want to be free?

Love

Love is a child,
Love is a need.
Love is a desire.
Love is a deed.

Love is a word.
Love is a home.
Love is a kiss.
Love is a poem.

Love is a friend.
Love is a heart.
Love is a must.
Love is a start

Love is to share.
It's a glorious trust.
Love is God.
His love for us.

Reach Out

To take a step...
            reach out
just a little, just enough
    to touch someone...
                somewhere
And someday...
    a touch will fill all things
only moments before...
            empty.
A word, a smile, an open hand...
        real and warm___
first friends, then...
            the cup fills as it will.
It's dangerous, it's risky, watchout...
        or you'll fall
deeper...
            into emptiness
What hope, but to step to the edge...
    to reach out and find
a higher level, more of myself, and maybe
        you.

One Breathless Moment

Oh, my heart is lonely with a need so great,
Oh, my heart is lonely for a love to share.
Not for love of money would I give my all,
But to have a love beyond compare.

Never before have I yearned so much
To feel a caress and a gentle touch;
Two lips they meet in a breathless moment
To tell each other what words cannot;
A love so true can be a blessing;
This kind of I need so much.

To Give Yourself

You were there for me, now I'm here for you
I'll always hold in my heart the love
   we once knew
To give of one's self when the other's in need
That's beautiful. So beautiful indeed.
To reach out with love, to family or foe,
To take time to understand, as we grow;
To live with concern, and not afraid to let it show
That's so beautiful. so beautiful indeed
To give of one's self. when someone's in need.

For You Only

Yesterday, I almost caught the rising sun
But. without thinking, I let it pass. someday
for you.
I'll reach out and catch it, hold it. and
never give it back. I'll keep it for
a while. for my very own. And then, in
some very special moment.
I'll offer it to you. No one else, just you.
Open your arms, extend. reach out, take
it. Yes only for you.

Love Me Twice

Love me for my kiss,
Love me for my smile.
Love me for my laughter,
Love me all the while.

Love me for my tears in vain
Love me for my sorrow;
Love me for my heart in pain,
Love me for tomorrow.

Tell me that you'll never leave,
So much pain in my heart
Will be brought on if you deceive me;
love me as from the start.

Love me with a rainbow,
Love me with sympathy;
Love me with a pot of gold
But most of all - love me
           for being me.

Never Alone

Some men say God's not alive.
But oh. if they only knew!
His the only artist that ever was
who paints the morning dew.
They can see Him in a falling star
and the beauty of a flower.
They surely know it must be Him
who takes back each fleeting hour

I thank you, Lord, for my new life.
and for dear friends you've sent to me.
But when my heart's heavy,
and my tears won't let me see.
You take my hand and squeeze it hard
and give me strength I need
To accept the heartaches in my life.
For all this. I humbly plead.

And Lord. help me to be patient.
When my hunger for things grow strong.
I know that if it's in your will
all of these things will come along.
Take now my life. and let it be
A window for your light;
Live in me and speak through me
That I'll guide others right.

Happy are
those who dream
dreams and are
ready to pay
the price to
make them
come true.

The most important thing of all
is love.
It will last forever.
When great deeds
are no longer possible,
love will endure
in small acts of kindness
toward the people around us.

If you love something,
  set it free.
If it comes back to you,
  it is yours.
If it doesn't,
  it never was.

These little red hearts
are sent from my heart...

In Memory Of.....

How long we live
is not for us to say.
We may have years ahead
or but a day.
The length of life
is not of our control.
But length is not
the measure of our soul.
Not length but width
and depth define the span
By which the Lord
takes measures of a man.
It matters not how long
before we sleep.
But only how wide
is our life - how deep.

"And remember!
I will be
with
you
always,
to
the
end
of the
age."

Matthew 28:20

I
can
complain
because
rose
bushes
have
thorns

or
rejoice
because
thorn
bushes
have
roses

Love

I pray that I may
learn from listening —
whether or not I agree
with what I hear.

As I have loved you, so you must love one
another. If you have love for one another,
then everyone will know that you are my
disciples. — John 13:34

I pray for the wisdom to realize
that progress begins only when I am
ready to detach myself from the idea
that I alone can control and solve
another's problem.

This is
the day which
the Lord
hath made.
　　　let us rejoice,
　　　　　and be glad
　　　　　in it.

God does not deprive us of His love;
we deprive him of our cooperation.
God would never reject us if we had
not rejected first His love. - St. Francis de Sales

Life is a measure to be filled —
　　not a cup to be drained.

A NEW KINg
Will ARISE

" When Christ who is
   our life shall appear,
then shall ye also
   appear with Him
      in glory."
                  Colossians 3:4

                  This is
            our joy —
      Christ our life
   here on earth, and
      for ever and ever
            in eternity.

Great is your gladness
and rich your Reward
When you make
your life's purpose
the choice of the Lord.

A Hug

A hug is like a warm sunny day,
bringing comfort to a lost or lonely soul

A hug can dry a tear,
increase a joy
fill an empty heart.

A hug can heal a hurt,
saying what no words can.
and understanding in any language.

A hug says, 'I care. You're ok.
Things will be all right. I love you.'

A hug fades distance. time. space.
the now of being two become one.
a common sharing.

Nothing can match the treasure of
common memories of trials endured
together. of quarrels and
Reconciliations and
generous emotions.

Up With People

Friends are like wine
they grow stronger with age

A smile can grow a mile

If you see someone without
a smile, give them one
of yours!

You Light Up My Life

Open your heart
    and let it be filled
with the good
    of the Lord.

Thoughts of You Today

"Every good and perfect gift is from above"

James 1:17

- What a perfect gift you are to me.

To a
Special Friend

You are
God's

garden
I Corinthians 3:9

-When I am with you
my faith grows.

You Are The Sunshine of My Life

My thoughts
are with you on
Your Birthday

- thoughts of love
of joy.
of thanks, to God
for making you.

God's love is everywhere...
especially in you.
HAPPY BIRTHDAY

Marriage Takes Three

I once thought marriage took
Just two to make a go
But now I am convinced
It takes the Lord also.
And not one marriage fails
Where Christ is asked to enter
As lovers come together
With Jesus at the center.
But marriage seldom thrives
And homes are incomplete
Till He is welcomed there
To help avent defeat.
In homes where God is first
It's obvious to see
Those unions really work,
For marriage still takes three.

Perry Tanksley

All
Around Us
We Can
See
the Glory
of
God

Love Is
All Around

Give
Thanks
to the
Lord
for He is
Good

No matter what
No matter where.
it's always home
if love is there.

God
bless
all
living
things.

Seek ye first
the Kingdom of God
and His
Righteousness
    Matthew 6:33

After your tears,
Love shall fill your emptiness
    (PSALM 126:5)

Let not your heart be troubled
    you believe in God.
    believe also in me.
        John 14:1

Whoever follows me...
Shall have the light of life.
    John 8:12

GRANDMOTHER

Strength and
honor are her
clothing ... she
openeth her mouth
with wisdom...
PROVERBS 31:25.26

Let not your heart be troubled
John 14:27

He has given purpose to lifes living
We walk by faith, not by sight
Corinthians 6:7

I am the way the truth and the Light
John 14:6

In every
    flower
He speaks
    of love
and beautiful
    tomorrows

Do not
mourn
what cannot
            Be;
Celebrate,
    rather,
what is, what was
and what will always be
and that is
the miracle of
His love
for us.

Let us
love one another
for love
is from God
and everyone
who loves
is born of God
and
knows Him.
John 4:7

PRAISE

the

LORD !

Beauty
is not discovered
with the eye ...
but with
the soul.

Those
who bring sunshine
in the lives
of others
cannot keep it
from themselves.
                    Sir James Barrie

Jesus

I met this man named Jesus
Who says he frees us
At first I had little belief
Now to my Relief
I've accepted the Lord,
So now I sing this chord.
"Glory, Glory, Praise Be to God."
Some think this is odd

But not me
I'm following the man with the key
Give all thanks to Him
His light is not dim
It goes out to all
Who answer the call
Of the blessed Lord Jesus
The one who really frees us

This man sent up his spirit
So all of us could hear it.
That salvation is not given
according to our standards of livin
It's given for what we believe
So that we'll never leave.
To each the holy spirit will give
What we need in order to live
First it gives us love
So we feel free like a dove.

Soon we get gifts
to give us lifts.
Soon we'll never fall
Instead we bounce back like a ball
So come on accept the ~~Holy~~ Spirit
And then let everyone hear it.

Ron

Let go and let God

Live all you can; it's a mistake not to.
It doesn't so much matter what you do
in particular, so long as you have your
life. If you haven't had that what have
you had?... What one loses one loses,
make no mistake about that.... The
right time is any time that one is
so lucky as to have.... Live!

God teach me to detach my mind from what others say and do, except to draw helpful lessons and guidance from them.

For there is a time... for every purpose and for every work.

God does not deprive us of His love: we deprive Him of our cooperation. God would never reject me if I had not first rejected His love.

If we say that we have no fault, we deceive ourselves and the truth is not in us.

We may think we can chance the things around us according to our desires. but when a solution does come. we find it was our desires that had changed.

God guide my thoughts and let these guide my actions.

I will make this day a happy one. for I alone can determine what kind of a day it will be.

What I can give is never as much as I get from the giving.

By love I do not mean natural tenderne
which is in people according to their
constitution, but I see it as a larger
principle of the soul, founded in reason
and spiritual understanding, which makes
us kind and gentle to all our fellow
creatures as ": creations of God.

William Law

Look to yourself - it is there that
all your answers are found.

"Why should we try to move mountains
with our own strength alone
when faith, 'even as a grain of
mustard seed', can help us achieve
what seemed impossible?"

Hold fast to dreams
for if dreams die.
Life is a broken-winged bird
that cannot fly.

Can Do

Did is a word of achievement.
Won't is a word of retreat.
Might is a word of
    bereavement.
Can't is a word of defeat.
Ought is a word of duty.
Try is a word of each hour.
Will is a word of beauty.
    Can is a word of power.

The Magic of Thinking Big

As one thinketh in his heart, so is he.

DAVID (Prophet)

Great men are those who see
that thoughts rule the world.

Emerson

The mind is its own place
and in itself
can make a heaven of hell
or a hell of heaven.

Milton

There is nothing either good or bad
except that thinking makes it so.

Shakespeare

Let a man seek virtue.
  and he will find wantonness.
Let him seek honor among men,
  and he will discover himself in a den of thieves.

Let him seek God in the world,
  and he will find nothingness.
Let him search for just a man,
  and he will find a bloody sword.

Let him cry for love unto the hearts of men,
  and hatred will answer.
Let him seek in the places of mankind for peace,
  and he will find himself among the dead.

Let him call unto the nations for truth,
  and falsehood and treachery will echo him.
But let him seek all goodness in himself,
  in humility and gentleness and faith,
  and he will see the face of God, and will
  find all the world arrayed in light and mercy.
And then, at last,
  he will no longer fear any man.

Don't Quit

When things go wrong, as they sometimes will,
When the road you're trudging seems all uphill,
When the funds are low and the debts are high,
And you want to smile, but you have to sigh,
When care is pressing you down a bit -
Rest if you must but don't you quit.

Life is queer with its twists and turns,
As everyone of us sometimes learns,
And many a person turns about
When they might have won had they stuck it out.
Don't give up though the pace seems slow -
You may succeed with another blow.

Often the struggler has given up
When he might have captured the victor's cup,
And when he learned too late
When the night came down
How close he was to the golden crown.

Success is failure turned inside out -
So stick to the fight when you're hardest hit, -
It's when things seem worst that you mustn't quit.

God's Love

God's love is like the rolling ocean
  So deep and very wide
No force can ever hope to check
  Or stop its surging tide.

Like craggy mountains towering upward.
  Vast and strong and tall.
There is no measure for His love
  And yet I have it all.

O. J. Robertson

The Rope

When a man
reaches the end
of his rope,

he comes to
the beginning
of God.

Edward A. Gloeggler

I Will Not Quit!

I will not quit until the battle's won;
I will not quit until I hear the words,

"Well done!"

Though rough be the way,
And hard be the fight,
I will not quit
the conflict and right!

There's much to be gained,
True choices to make...

Lord, show me the path—
Just the right one
to take!

Roxie Lusk Smith

I want to share my joy with you...
his name is Jesus.

Christmas is very special ...
when you know Jesus

Life pauses for a moment
of love at Christmas -
When in a certain still moment
love is born within us,
then we know the true
meaning of Christmas.

Joy - Love - Peace
May you discover the joy
of giving. the love in sharing.
the peace in living.

I go out
all the time
with so many
people
but when "I
need someone to
understand me
it is not to
these acquaintances
that I turn
it is
always to you"
my true friend.

Susan Polis Schultz

This is all I ask

Lord, show me the way
I can somehow repay
The blessings you've given to me...
Lord, teach me to do
What you want me to
And to be what you want me to be...
I'm unworthy, I know
But I do love you so—
I beg you to answer my plea.
I've not much to give
But as long as I live
May I give it completely
                    to thee!

The Only Way to Have a Friend

The only way to have a friend
  Is to be one yourself,
The only way to keep a friend
  Is to give from that wealth.

For friendship must be doublefold,
  Each one must give his share
Of feelings true if he would reap
  The blessings that are there.

If you would say, "He is my friend,"
  Then nothing else will do
But you must say, "I am his friend,"
  And prove that fact be true.

Peace

With eager heart and will on fire,
I fought to win my great desire.
"Peace shall be mine," I said; but life
Grew bitter in the weary strife.

My soul was tired, and my pride
Was wounded deep: to Heaven I cried,
"God grant me peace or I must die,"
The dumb star glittered no reply.

Broken at last, I bowed my head,
Forgetting all myself, and said,
"Whatever comes, His will be done,"
And in that moment peace was won.

Henry Van Dyke

Success

Success is speaking words of praise,
In cheering other people's ways,
In doing just the best you can.
With every task and every plan.
It's silence when your speech would hurt,
Politeness when your neighbor's curt.
It's deafness when the scandal flows,
And sympathy with others' woes.
It's loyalty when duty calls,
It's courage when disaster falls,
It's patience when the hours are long,
It's found in laughter and in song,
It's in the silent time of prayer.
In happiness and in despair,
In all of life and nothing less
We find the things we call success.

No Regrets

Isn't it good at the end of the day
To look up to God and be able to say
"Dear Lord, I helped someone today."
But isn't it sad if instead you must say
"Dear Lord, I hurt someone today."
I drove the nails a little bit deeper
And forgot that I am my brother's keeper."

Isn't it better when the day is done
To know that you have injured no one.
From the time of your waking,
Till you lie down to sleep.
Remember the promises that we should keep,
To love one another as He loves us too,
And you'll never regret any good that you do.

Barbara Zepp

Home

Home is where the heart is,
  you have often heard it said.
Home is where the songbirds sing
  their sweetest, overhead.

Home is like the rainbow's end
  that beckons in the blue.
Home is where your brightest dreams
  take root and all come true.

And yet it's more than just a place
  where people sleep and eat.
A home that's real has something
  indefinable and sweet.

It may be just a cottage,
  or a castle with a dome.
But if God dwells within its walls
  it really is a Home!

Nick Kenny

The Artist

I love to watch
God paint the dawn
In scarlet flush and gold;
I love to watch
Him touch the sky
In colors bright and bold.
I love to watch
God paint the dusk
In purple- shadowed gray.
Then leave His name
upon it all -
Artist of night and day!

Marion Schoeberlein

The
highest Good

To attain the highest good
Of true man and womanhood.
Simply do
your honest best -
God with joy
will do the rest

James Riley

To believe in God
Is to know that
all the rules are fair
and that there will
be wonderful surprises

The most beautiful things
of the world are not
seen with the eyes
but felt with the heart

The best things can never be kept
they must be given away;
a smile, a kiss and love.

You have touched me;
I have grown

a friend is a special blessing

Love wasn't put in your heart to stay
Love isn't love til you give it away

anxious hearts are heavy,
but a word of encouragement
does wonders.

PROV 12

Each new friend makes
the world a little brighter

I want to share my joy with you...
his name is Jesus

Don't walk in front of me, I may not follow
Don't walk in behind me, I may not lead
Just walk beside me and be my friend

Joy - Love - Peace

May you discover the joy of giving
the love in sharing,
the peace in living.

If you love something, set it free.
If it comes back to you, it is yours.
If it doesn't, it never was.

There are many shells
      on the beach
            and yet
each one is individual.

Each is fitted and formed
      by its own life.

For one cannot collect
      all the beautiful shells
            on the beach.

One can collect only a few.
      and they are more beautiful
            if they are few.
                  ANNE MORROW LINDBERGH

            Therese & Fritz
            Sept. 6. 1980

"Now Daddy is part of God.
I guess when you die you
become much more bigger
because you're part of everything"

Sean Lennon. Age 5
On the death of his father.
John Lennon

I am an idea
Conceived in the mind of the Universe
And interpreted in the minds
of the individuals I meet

Within myself I am constant
Yet I am as ever changing
As the people who interpret me

I can control my actions
But I can not control their thoughts
Therefore. I must do what I think right
And let others—
Think what they will

Life comes in the form of opportunities
which are easy to recognize
- once they have been wasted

It starts
At a time called birth
and continues
Till a time called death
It is called Life
It comes with no guarantees
"If 60 years or 60 thousand miles
whichever comes first."
And somehow
They've even left the instructions out
Yes, all we get
Is Life itself
And it's up to us
To do the living

Lord- Please, quick
Give me a line,
    or something to say
That might start to explain
The storm raging inside me
    since she walked into the room
Just one line that will let her (him) know
The feelings deep in my heart

In my lifetime
    I hope to develop
Arms that are strong
    Hands that are gentle
Ears that will listen
    Eyes that are kind
A tongue that will speak softly
    A mind full of wisdom
    A heart that understands

I would not ask from you
anything that you were not capable
of giving
I would not ask from you
anything but that which I truly need
And I would not take from you
Without giving equal value in return

Should I hesitate as I speak
Please don't think me preoccupied
For words don't come easily
When one really cares
And too often I evaluate each word
Trying to be anyone
    —but myself

And the fear of rejection
    Brings confusion
The confusion brings silence
And my heart prays
    That you might hear my silence
    —and understand

Listen carefully, to the words of others
For often very deep truths are revealed
    clothed in jest

How often the world introduces
People we never get to know
They walk right in, we see their smile
Then watch as they turn and go

We stand and scan the footprints
Their leaving left behind
And the departure of a stranger
Can leave footprints in the mind

Footprints
Four footprints in the sand
Waves washing to shore
The moon hiding behind flourescent clouds
A star for wishing
Indentions in the sand of two people
        huddled close
    Silence - and yet conversation
    The chill of the wind blowing in from sea
    Lights on distant ships
    Hands -
        Holding -
            Touching -
                Caressing -
The sun awakening across the horizon
Footprints
Four footprints running in the sun
As if tomorrow could never come
Laughter
    a feeling of Happiness - deep inside
    Living Life
            Giving
                Sharing
        Tomorrow
        Footprints
        Two footprints in the sand
                Searching
                Remembering

There are so many words
    Yet there are no words
For when I look into your eyes
    No words need to be spoken
    And how could I ever try to explain
        The trembling in my body
        When I touch your face

There are no words to explain an emotion
    So I open to you my mind
        That you might walk
Among my Dreams and Memories
    Then ... and only then
    You might understand my silence

Whether it was chance
   Or that thing called fate
      That brought you to me
I really can't say,
      and I don't believe
         It really matters

For I have been lucky enough
To have the opportunity to hold you
Not just in my arms
But also in my heart

And should the winds of time
      Blow hard enough
         To take you from my arms

You can rest assured
      They will never
         Take you from my heart

Many days have come and gone
Since the day you shared with me
It was Our Day
A Red Letter Day for me

We shared much more than just time
Laughter -
Conversation -
Silence -

You gave me reason to smile again
and be excited about tomorrow

Now, when saddness surrounds me
That you were gone so soon
I try to rejoice
That you ever came at all

If I were to take stock
Of all my worldly treasures
The memories I have
Of the few hours spent with you
Would be my most cherished
                    possessions

Because I took a moment to speak
and you took a second to smile
A tiny part of me will leave with
and a little bit of you will stay you

Today
Someone asked me
If I had forgotten you
With a moments thought and a subtle smile
I answered no

No, I haven't forgotten
The years we shared
When you gave to me
And I gave to you
And like everything else in life
Some was good
Some was bad

But to completely forget
Would create a void in my life

So even as I say
I'm over you
I have strength to choose
Not to forget you

The time of my life
In relation to the world
In insignificant

The time spent with you
In relation to my life
Was brief –
        but not insignificant

You came into my life
        Unannounced
            Uninvited
                But not unwanted
You came at a time that I needed
    A tender smile
            A gentle touch
                A woman's (man's) company
You came with understanding
        For you asked no questions
With loving care
        You healed my wounds
            And nursed me to health again
Then you watched over me
            Till I regained my courage
                To face the world again
And in your wisdom you realized
        My need to be free
            So you tied no bounds
Now each night
        Wherever I am
I think of you
        Wherever you are
And in my heart I repeat
        "Thank you"

This page is written especially
for those of you
who read the last page first.
If by chance, this applies to you
then you have found a special book
that will be cherished many years.